the true book of

PLANT EXPERIMENTS
By Illa Podendorf

Dozens of simple experiments—
with plants and parts of plants
—which children can do at home
or at school.

Miss Podendorf begins simply
with touch-and-tell experiments
to give a concept of parts of
plants.

Then there are experiments with
seeds, green plants, and spore
plants. By seeing and doing, children learn what is true and, just
as important, what is not true.

This book grew from Illa Podendorf's experience in teaching
science to children in the Laboratory School, University of Chicago.

The "true book" series is prepared
under the direction of
Illa Podendorf
Laboratory School, University of Chicago
Ninety-eight per cent of the text is in words from
the *Combined Word List for Primary Reading*

the true book of

Plant

xperiments

by ILLA PODENDORF

pictures by BILL ARMSTRONG

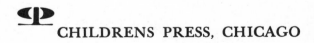 CHILDRENS PRESS, CHICAGO

IN THIS BOOK

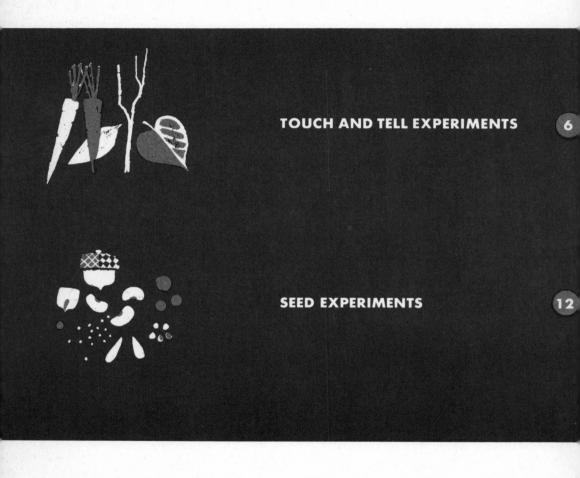

Library of Congress Catalog Card Number: 60-66

3 4 5 6 7 8 9 10 11 12 13 14 15 16 17 18 19 20 21 22 23 24 25   R   75 74 73 72 71 70 69 6

Most green plants have

roots,   stems,   leaves,

flowers and seeds.

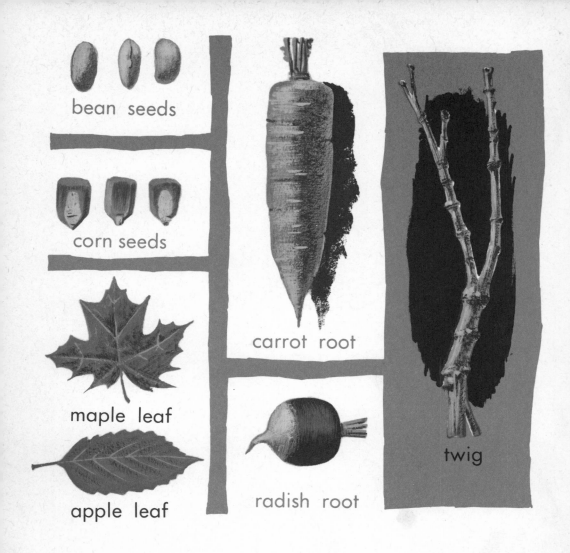

bean seeds

corn seeds

carrot root

maple leaf

apple leaf

radish root

twig

Nancy and Jane played
Touch-and-Tell with these
parts of plants.

8

Nancy put one of the plant
parts in a box. Jane did not
see which one it was.

Jane put her hand in the box
and touched the part. She said
she knew it was a root because
of the shape, and she was right.
It was the carrot root in the box.

Nancy and Jane learned many things about leaves.

They touched the leaves and looked at them carefully.

The elm leaf was rough. The cottonwood leaf was smooth. The oak leaf was lobed. The ash leaf had many parts to it.

ELM LEAF

COTTONWOOD LEAF

OAK LEAF

Nancy and Jane played Touch-and-Tell with leaves.

Nancy and Jane played Touch-and-Tell with flowers. The fragrance of the flowers helped them, too.

David did an experiment with twelve bean seeds. He put six bean seeds in water one evening. In the morning, the six bean seeds which were in water looked larger than the others which were not put in water. David placed them side by side in two rows to see if they really were bigger.

David could see a little hole in the seed's coat. Maybe the water went in through the little hole, he thought.

David could see a little scar, too.

The seeds that had been
in water were softer, wrinkled
and bigger.

David opened one of them
and another one, and another
one.

This is what he saw.

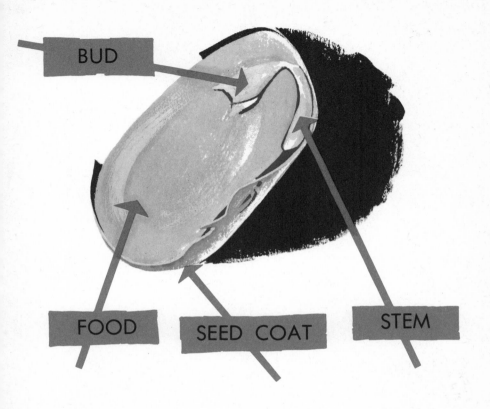

BUD

FOOD SEED COAT STEM

All seeds are alike in two important ways. They have very young plants in them. They have food for the young plants in them.

David did an
experiment with
more bean seeds.
He put dirt
in a flower pot.
He placed three
bean seeds on top of the dirt.
He covered them with more
dirt. He watered the seeds
well and put them in a window.

The sun shone on David's
experiment. In a few days he
could see the seeds had started
to grow. When a seed begins
to grow we say it *germinates*.

David did another experiment.

He planted three bean seeds in one flower pot and three bean seeds in another flower pot.

He treated them the same, except for one thing. He did not water the seeds in one of the flower pots.

The seeds in the flower pot that was not watered did not germinate. The others did. He decided that plants need water to germinate.

David used two more flower pots. He planted three bean seeds in each of them. He watered both of them with the same amount of water.

He put one in a warm, dark place. He put the other in a warm, light place. The seeds in both pots germinated.

David decided that seeds do not need light to begin to grow.

David had learned that seeds need water and warmth to germinate.

"Do they need rich soil to germinate?" his father asked.

David decided to find out.

He planted six seeds in sand
and six seeds in good soil and
watered them with the same amount
of water. In a few days the seeds
in both pots were growing.

Seeds do not need rich soil
to germinate.

David wished he could see
what happened under the sand.
His father showed him how
to plant radish seeds on a
wet piece of blotting paper
and cover them with a piece
of glass.

David watched the seeds
as they began to grow.

David found another way to plant seeds so that he could watch them germinate.

He folded a piece of paper towel into a cone so that no dirt could fall out of it. He put it in a glass funnel. Sand was put in the paper.

Then David put corn and bean seeds between the paper and the glass.

Each day, David watered the sand.

The seeds began to grow.
He thought he could see the
tiny leaves, stems, roots and
root hairs.

Young bean plants bend their stems and push their way up. They use the food in the seeds as they germinate and grow.

After young bean plants are up, they lift two leaves toward the sunlight. The two halves of the bean seeds come up with the leaves.

Young corn plants do not bend their stems as they come up. Young corn plants push their way up with a rolled-up leaf. They use the food in the seeds as they germinate and grow.

David found two pieces of
glass about four inches square.
He laid a piece of blotting
paper, the same size, on one
of the pieces of glass.

Then he put the seeds on
the piece of blotter. He
covered it with the other
piece of glass and put a
rubber band around it.

Then he stood the glass on
end in water against a glass
jar for support.

The water moved up in the
blotter and touched the seeds.
The seeds began to grow.
Then David played a trick.

He turned the glass upside
down.

The roots turned and grew
toward the water. The leaves
turned and grew toward the sun.

After a few days it looked
like this.

Green plants need sunshine, water and good soil to keep them growing.

David wondered how water went from the soil into the plant.

He colored some water with green ink and placed a carrot in it.

A few hours later, he cut
the carrot. He could see
where the colored water had
gone.

David put a stick of celery
in a glass of water with brown
ink. It looked like this the
next morning.

David did this experiment
with another celery stalk.

He split the stalk part way up.

He put one part of the celery
in green water. He put the
other part in brown water.

There are small tubes in
plant stems and roots. The
water goes up the tubes to
the leaves.

Try this experiment
with red ink or food
coloring in the water.

The water which goes into the roots from the soil has important minerals in it.

The water takes the minerals from the soil.

Sometimes soil is not good because it does not have enough of the important minerals in it.

Plants which grow in poor soil are often weak.

David and his mother put some plant food minerals in water.

They watered the plants with the water with minerals in it. They hoped the plants would be strong and healthy.

Some plants which have seeds
have other ways to get new
plants.

Peggy found a plant that would
grow from a stem. She put a
stem in water until it got roots.

Then she put the part with
roots on it in dirt.

Peggy found some grass that
grew from underground stems.
Grass may grow from seeds, too.

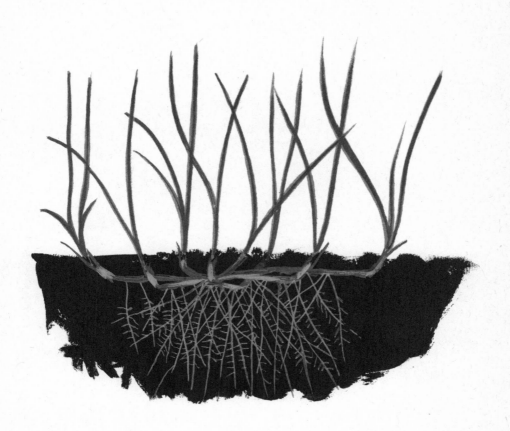

Sometimes new plants grow on leaves. This is a leaf with tiny new plants on it.

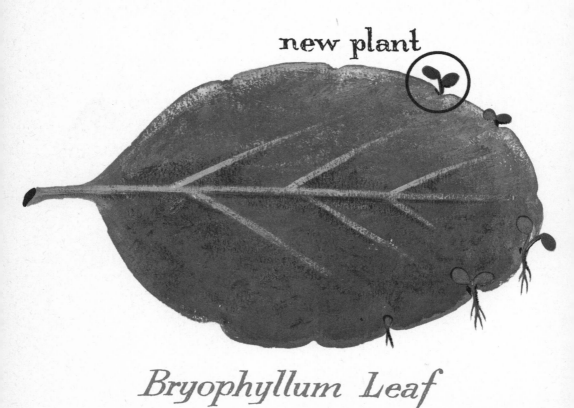

new plant

Bryophyllum Leaf

Peggy put a part of a carrot root in water. It grew a new top.

A sweet potato, with part of it in water, will grow a new vine.

Ferns

Mosses

Nancy found these woodland plants. None of these plants have seeds. Their new plants grow from spores. The spores are so tiny that they are hard to see. Many spores together look like dust.

Lichens

Nancy made a terrarium. A terrarium is a tiny woodland in a glass bowl.

She gathered fresh soil from the woods.

She put some of it in the bottom of her glass bowl. She made the soil about two inches deep.

She put different kinds of woodland plants on the soil.

Then she watered it well and put a glass over the top.

She will not need to water it for a long time.

All of these plants are not
green.

All of them have spores.

Nancy made a print of the spores of a mushroom.

She covered a card with a thin layer of rubber cement. She let it dry a bit. She put the mushroom cup down on the card. The mushroom was ready to drop its spores. It dropped them on the rubber cement on the card. The spores stuck fast.

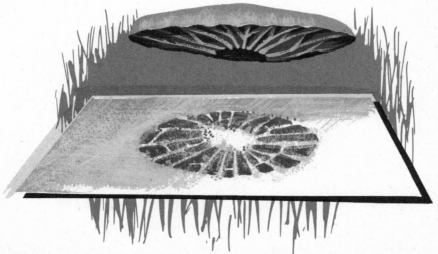

Nancy found a puffball near the woods. A puffball is a plant. It is never green. It has spores instead of seeds.

Puffballs have many spores. The spores look like dust. There are too many to count.

Nancy looked at some spores through a microscope.

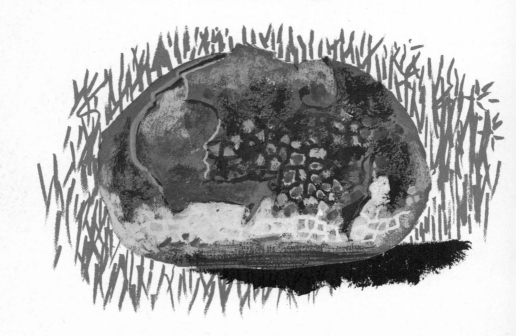

SOME THINGS TO DO

1. Do the experiments in this book for yourself.
2. Plan an experiment to find if a plant needs soil to grow for a long time.
3. Plan an experiment to show if a plant needs light to grow for a long time.
4. Plan an experiment to see if a seed will germinate in a cold place.
5. Plan a way to find out if corn or radish seeds get bigger when they are put in water.
6. Find out how many seeds there are in a cherry, an apple and a cantaloupe.